GODDESS; EVOLUTION OF

BY TGODDESS

Table of Contents

I AM

I am the girl with the afro
I am the girl with the gap in between her teeth
I am the girl with the scar that's on the left side of her cheek
I am brown
More like that caramel cake brown

You know
That caramel cake
That your grandma bake
Every christmas and thanksgiving day
That's the perfect taste
Of my brown skin

I am the girl with the eyes
Who can see beneath the lies
I am the girl with the mouth
Who loves to speak
But can be quiet if needed to be

I am a product of a single mother
whose mother was a single mother
whose mothers mother was aahh....

aahh.... Wait

That's as far as I could go
Because honestly
I don't fucking know

I am a product of a absent dad
Whose dad was an absent dad
Whose dad's dad might have been an absent dad

I know, I know
It sounds sad

But I am optimistic
Also realistic
A divine beauty
Who understands
Empathy
But can give

Two fucks
About someone's
Sympathy

I am the painter
Of the picture
I want to be

I am not my parents mistakes
I am not just another brown face

I am a force of nature
making life my bitch
A goddess that is known
for her many tricks

I bathe in the water of confidence
I soak in the bubbles of love

So scars of my past
No longer exists

Because I
Yes me, who could only define me,
have taken control of my own DESTINY

LOVE

Love is more than just a word
Love is POWERFUL
Love is ENERGY

That will have your heart open
Fiending for affections
To replace the loneliness
The pain
It creates a sense of hope
for better days

Love is more than just a word

Don't know how it begins,
Fearful on how it will end
Aware that it starts from within

Hoping that love will be in the air
With each breath intake
I inhale the the fresh air
The fresh air of LOVE

LOVE POWER

The power of love
An energy that is triggered by emotions
An energy that is triggered by another
A man and a woman
A child and a mother

The power of love
is a beautiful feeling

With the right ingredients

Sprinkle it with the feeling of joy
Sprinkle it with the feeling of honesty
It creates a trust feeling
That is shared
Showing the power of love

Love

What a powerful energy

It can have a negative effect

With the wrong ingredients

A beautiful disaster
Created by the master
Who abuse the power of love

Don't underestimate
The power of love

HE NEEDS ME

I stayed
I stayed because part of me
Believed things will be different

I stayed
Because the amount of faith I had in him
I just knew he was going to change

I stayed
Because I understand his pain
I wanted to be the light
That shine on his darkest days

I stayed
Because I had this idea
That one day I will marry a black men
Have cute little black babies
And live the black American dream

I stayed
Because he needs me
He needs me
I know he do
It's hard for a black men
But what they fail to realize
It's hard on us black women to

I used to take the focus off me
put it all into you
thinking of ways
to heal a black man's pain
While sinking into
the black woman's blues

But he needs me
I know he do

How can I shower him
With the love that he needs
If I lack that love from

Within me?

 How can I?

Self love
Self care
Self love
Self care
Self love
Self care...?

My subconscious speaks
But I ignore me
tending to his every needs

Planting the seeds of his confidence
But slowly draining me

He needs me
Even though
Deep down I know
I need me too

HE DOESN'T LOVE YOU

He doesn't love you
He refuses to pick the rose
from concrete but chooses
to step on every crack

With no care in the world
Of breaking his momma back

He doesn't love you
Damaged and confused
On what to do
With a gem
As beautiful as you

Clear and pure
His only wish is
to misuse

See

He probably grew up in a home
Where love was never shown
Incapable of
Giving you the love
You need

He doesn't love you
But lust over
The fantasies

Of creating
The family he feels he needs
So he doesn't see
The damage he does

Blindly confused
Of his wants

He steps on the rose
Growing from the concrete

Which is YOU
A beautiful vibrant RED

The only rose
Where dandelion grows

Waiting to get picked
By the man
Who doesn't know or understand
LOVE

Piling up the broken sticks
That has fallen from his
tree's foundation

He didn't see the rose
In between

The burdens of life
Derailed him from the love
of his life

Detached away from his feminine
side casting you away
Blocking the sun and causing the rain

Where the rose will remain
But never grow
In the arms of man
Who only know sorrow

POWER YOU HAVE OVER ME

The power you have over me
Because of the love I have for you
Will soon go out of use

I gave you my all
And you reciprocated it
With your verbal abuse

The power you have over me
Because of the love I have for you
Will soon go out of use

Because baby

Once I stop caring
It will be no more sharing
My heart
It will no longer
Have a soft spot
For you

The power you have over me
Will soon expire
for you took my heart, my soul,
my desires
you used them as if they were
your favorite pawns

As I just foolishly sat there
Playing my role

I will no longer make that same move
I will no longer make that same excuse

Time after time I believe the lies

But yet nothing has changed

You told me if I was a true women,
I would hold you down
You told me if I was true to you
You will give me the world

You told me if I was true to you

That I will forever be your girl

It didn't click to me then
Not once did you say
All the things that you
Will do on your end

To love me
To cherish me
To keep me

But

Yet you wanted to be treated
As if you were a king

You took advantage
Of my GODDESS ways
And treated me as if
I'm not your woman
But your own personal slave

YEAHH...

You will no longer
Have that POWER over me

LOVE VICTIM

I survived his love
Tied down by his lies
His soft lips
Spoke words
That broke and eased me
All at the same time

Blinded by his trauma I allowed

My mind
My body
My soul
To submit
Giving him permission to hit

And which each blow
Came more lies
Disrespect
Leaving scars on the inside
That can not easily be repatched

I am a victim of love
Overdosing
From the idea of
Being in love

I fell victim to his schemes
and what seemed
Like a beautiful ending

Suffering to stay
While my trust began
To drain away

Allowing his love
to drive me insane
A feeling that
I can't escape
I love him
I know I have to leave

But why does it seem
as if his love
doesnt love me?

Knotting up the ropes
So I couldn't break free
Trapped in his cycle
Traits of toxicity

Blinded by his sweet facades
The deceptions of change
Knowing that I need to get
the fuck away

I can't deny
What I feel inside
Being a victim of
his love and lies
I realize, enduring so much pain,
I have to survive
Survive his LOVE

LOVE VICTIM PART 2

I am a victim of love
I was held hostage by affections
Soft lips spoke words
That kissed and licked me
So gentle
From my forehead to my toes

I was hypnotized
glorifying the feeling
that I get
When I get a hit
of your love

Tied down by trust
Knotting up the ropes
so I couldn't break free
His ears belongs to me
and he listen when I speak

I can't deny
What I feel inside
Being a victim of his LOVE
Has soften me

As I look into my lovers eyes
Feet tied down by trust
A bond that was only for us

He got me
I got him
His ying to his yang
My twinflame
Has captured me
With his LOVE

HIS EYES

His eyes was the key to his soul
Giving away his true self
Buried in the emotions inside
A glimpse of his eyes

Which tells no lies
Lets me know
Just how he feels within

When he looks at me
With love in his eyes
I get a chance to
To see how he feels inside

Fantasizing about our
love and how it only gets
fine like wine with time

When he looks at me
I can tell that he knows
I am the one he wants to greet
In the morning next to the sun

He peeks through the window
Of my soul
When he look at me
With those eyes

He lets me know its okay
To show my vulnerable side
When he looks at me
I know I'm safe in his eyes
Which, I feel, can tell no lies

FIRST MOVE

The thoughts of you
Brings me back to a time
of when we first locked eyes

See normally I don't
make the first move
But when I saw you
from across the room
I notice you were eying me
eyeing you

As we let our eye speak
I couldn't help but think

I imagine us on the beach
Listening to nature sing
as the sky paints a picture
Using clouds as it theme

Immersed in your presence
While the sun beam
On our beautiful brown skin
Leisurely, basking it all in

See normally I don't make move
Just like you
I enjoyed what my eyes
perceived

So I decided to break
The silence
And walk up to my
Future bae…
I mean future husband

Excuse me mister dark skin
What is your name ?
Normally
I don't make the first move

But for you
I'm willing to make a change

LOVE THROUGH CLOUDY DAYS

My love runs deep
Deeper than the memories
Within your head
Deeper than the deep blue sea

My love doesnt fade
On them cloudy days
When it begins to rain

When emotions become
filled with range
Full of heartaches
When it begins to pour
Love covers me
with the perfect umbrella
Love is my cure

As the clouds
Begins to fade away
The sun appears
Bringing more color
On this supposedly
gloomy day

Love will never fade away
But them cloudy days WILL

DEAR GODDESS

Dear goddess,
You are a goddess
Only a god can handle

A queen whose throne
Is only made for a king

A woman whose time
Shouldn't be consumed
tending to grown boys
But used wisely
accompanied by a grown men

LOVE IS A POWERFUL ENERGY

It triggers emotions. Sometimes us humans can not deal with emotions or simply can not process them in a healthy manner. Once we feel as if our love is being misused or in some cases abused we tend to shut the door on love. Not realizing that love starts from within and shines brightly without. Love brings beauty to life. Love is beauty itself. Love is an energy that pulls you in ready to give you life! The type of love you exchange shows the type of love you will receive. Love is more than just a word. Its abundance and joy. Why, love is a powerful energy.

NIA

Her smiles gets to me
everytime
Her curiosity gets
the best of me

I see her little eyes
watching me

One day her actions
Will show
The reflections of me
As she grows
into the bright light
That will shine
So bright
Glowing
In her destiny

LOST

On the road to success
But yet my feet won't move
It's like i'm stuck in quicksand
Life I barely have a clue

I have hope
Picking up the broken pieces
That I have broke

Lost in this world
Yet I have faith
The pain and sorrows
will soon fade away

They say if you strive
You will see better days
No guidelines through
struggles
Sometimes the lemons
Were to sour for my taste

Lost in this world
Yet I carry love
Thriving above
The I cants
Leaving them

In the hands
of the one above

Knowing that my destiny
depends on me
Despite the direction
I shall succeed

HOLDING ON

What are you holding on to?

Yea I get it..
You in love

But wasn't you the one
Complaining on how
they just don't
get you?..

I see your actions is reflecting

The pain that relationship
must have caused you.

What are you holding on to?

Trust me I get it
I was once stuck at job
That i hated so much

I stayed of course
Rent needed to be paid
And I needed to eat

But let's be real
I know people
was tired of me complaining

Shit!
Even I was sick of me

What are you holding on to?

Just letting time pass you by
Using excuses
As your reasons why
You had big dreams

Dreams that you can achieve
If you stop speaking
Down upon yourself

Blocking out the negative

Rather its people
places and or things

What are you holding on to?

I know and you know
That it's time to let go

Let it go
It no longer serves you.

THE LIGHT THAT SHINES BRIGHT

Hold on to that light
The light that shines
Bright within

In a world
where darkness
seems to win

That light
Your light

The flame
that sparks up
a gloomy room

That light
Your light

The one that inspire others
to shine
Just like you

Hold on to the light
Your light
The one that makes
You YOU

UNIVERSE SPEAKS

Fuck !

Back at square one
I could've sworn
I made it to square two

Defeated square three
Skip over square four
And landed on square five

Now it seems as if
my life put itself
in rewind

I could have took
It as the universe
giving me signs

But instead
I stayed in my room
Balled up
and cried

Knowing damn well
I wanted to
Hit a homerun
And get the fuck
Off of first base

Blinded by
my stubborn ways
Still a slave
To my emotions
An opp towards
my gut feeling

I dive deeper
into the lies

That was created

So I REPEAT

Falling on my ass
Instead of
landing on my feet

Sometimes I feel
As if the universe
Is truly fucking
with me

When the universe speaks

It makes you repeat

Til one day
The vision become
clear as a crystal
And there is no need

CLEAR MIND

My mind has no
more room for
mistakes

My heart likes to fight

Allowing my gut
to get me back
right

I repeat

To myself daily
No more room
For mistakes

Angry
Sadness
Pain

Was my daily
meals as my
feelings begins
to pile up
On my plate

I repeat

No more room
for mistakes

My mind has
no more room
for mistakes

Washing it down
With the sweet
juices of gratitude
and love

Understanding the
power of the words
If there's a will

there's a way

Taking the lessons
and enjoying
the blessings

Of the choices
That I made

FIRE WITHIN

She remembers

Burning that fire within
taking that range

That pain
The burdens
She endured from life

She made fire

Flames that touches
the stars
and light up
the sky
day or night

Colors of yellow and
orange

Showed the trails
of her pathway

Filled with fuels
Even far away
You will still
feel and see
the power of her
flames

Determinations
Was deep in
Her veins

Channeling in
her inner strength
To get through
the truth of life

She could no longer
turn a blind eye

Madness and sadness
played a role
Casting her out

Waking her up
from this dream of fear
The power of her flames
Spark fire into
the listening ears

She no longer
dwell over the struggles of life
Instead bringing the light
To the fire of her flames

Understanding that
If there's a will there's a way

In order to see true
change it starts from
within

Controlling the flames
of her FIRE
She remembered
and mastered
The flames within

HER LOVE

She gave her love
Her love was filled
with light

Brightening up the sky
From town to town
City to city
State to state

Giving earth
the lightning it needs
on its darkest days

She gave birth
that created earth

Trails of her feminine ways
made its way into
the hearts of the yangs
Being its ying

Birthing human-beings
That populates from
Town to town
City to city
State to state

She brings a perfect touch
of harmony and love

Dipped in gold
Warrior of the souls

She is you
She is me
She is every women
Dip in divine energy

Torn in-between
but yet
staying true
to her destiny

She knows
She is a queen
And should be
Valued as such
It is a must

Her heart
makes her
easy to trust

Her ears
Is open to listen
To the cries of her
children
her neighbor
To anyone
who comes near